RODNEY RICHARDS

POETS SING HAPPY POEMS

In an era of chaos

IMPORTANT NOTICES

Trade print ISBN 979-8990453630

eBook ISBN 979-8990453647

Cover by Jesse Richards, author/artist of *Unknown New York* and others
https://www.jesserichards.com/shelf/

Published by ABLiA Media LLC, Hamilton NJ USA

Disclaimers

Guest contributors' poems are identified by author name and have granted permission to only use their poems and Bios for this book. The author's and contributors' expressed opinions or views may reflect earlier times or may change. Some events and descriptions are real, others use poetic license or may be contrived or imagined.

All poems composed by Rodney Richards, author, are identified by poem title only.

The Secretariat of the Universal House of Justice has granted permission to use Bahá'í texts freely. Photos are owned or licensed by the author, are in the public domain, are free to use, maybe from a contributor, or are from CC Commons et al.

Any company names or product/brand names are registered and/or trademarked by their respective companies.

AI was not used to create or modify content.

Contents

DEDICATED TO

Those who are unhappy.

I can't imagine how hard it is to find a glimmer of hope or joy in difficult circumstances or under conditions that sadden us. Some things happening now, and those in the past, horrible. The future for too many looks bleak. Some lose hope. As long as we are alive, despair is a soul-killer. It leads nowhere.

In America, suicide is the 11th leading cause of death, over 49,000 in 2022. Guns cause over 50% of them. But 94% of Americans say suicide can be prevented. So can wars.

It's difficult to remember that it's not how the world treats you, but how you deal with it that counts. We have the power to change our condition in some instances, not others.

There is an overused cliché but true, God is ready to help. As Jesus said, "Knock, and the door shall open." When something scares or depresses me, I pray "Oh God, guide me." This 1883 portion of a sonnet by Emma Lazarus fills me with the hopeful promise of a better today:

Give me your tired, your poor,
Your huddled masses yearning to breathe free,
The wretched refuse of your teeming shore.
Send these, the homeless, tempest-tost to me,
I lift my lamp beside the golden door!

I'll add, "To welcome and shelter thee."

Hope, like the huge, yellow-muted monarch butterfly, represents beauty and freedom. Hope, the mystic phoenix, rises from the ashes of lost causes, changes the situation or your circumstance, and effects the world around you, for the better. Hope has the power and strength to change attitudes and make things brighter, right now, today.

Hope is the Holy Spirit in action, alive in us all.
Raise your glass to hope and spirit, "Here! Here!"
Cheers bring joy, laughter, and singing.

THIS IS THE WORLD
      I WANT TO LIVE IN.
   The Shared World.

National Poetry Month April 2025

Artwork by Christy Mandin. Lines excerpted from the poem "Gate A-4" by Naomi Shihab Nye, from Honeybee (Greenwillow Books, an imprint of HarperCollins Publishers, 2008). For more free poetry resources, visit: Poets.org/npm

Shout outs to National Poetry Month in the USA, April, and the Academy of American Poets. Kudos to all organizations, educators, and persons that promote poetry.

INTRODUCTION

Live! Love! Laugh! Sing! Why not? What day do you wait for? You might be dead tomorrow; how would you like to be remembered?

The ephemeral or abstract versus real and tangible. Both exist, coexist, intertwine, and mix in this contingent world we call Earth, the third planet from the fixed star we call Sol.

In 2025 people suffer from debilitating troubles of every type and range. Physical, emotional, mental, and spiritual pain affects vast majority of people. But even in pain, our spirit can smile.

The words "smile," "laugh" and "love," are abstract, language representations of how muscles in our tongue, lips, and face move. Language or words, sounds and their combinations are abstract also, and go back ages to man's earliest grunts. We have over 7,000 languages and dialects in 142 basic language groups. Add thousands of physical expressions, face, hand, arm, or body movements and *Voila!* fantastic communication.

We live for human-to-human interaction.

That human touch we had in the womb and the thrum of our mother's body as she sang us a lullaby remains within forever. Sound is touch too. Words and musical notes sit on the page yet resonate in our mind, reach our spirit and we can't help nodding, tapping our fingers, or rising and dancing. Words and music are heart to heart, mind to mind, soul to soul, spirit to spirit, just like touch is. They are ladders to our soul. We climb the rungs to reach nirvana.

Once reached, natural, unbidden, innate, our soul cannot help responding. Here are a few of my word songs, and those of others, that I hope create those rungs sought.

"Now is the time to cheer and refresh the down-cast through the invigorating breeze of love and fellowship, and the living waters of friendliness and charity."
—Bahá'u'lláh, *Gleanings from the Writings of Bahá'u'lláh*

Live happy

"Happiness is a psychological condition
created in brain, mind and heart,
the effect of which works out
from the centre
to the circumference."

'Abdu'l-Bahá, the Center of Bahá'u'lláh's Covenant

Happiness runs in a circular motion, as Donovan sang.

People are people

Give 'em half a chance
they crave your smiles, peace, love too.
Laughter binds hearts like glue

The Gift of Poetry

Lives in every heartbeat, every person
releases music, words, songs, accapella coordination
The art of voice made for sight, touch, inhalation
flooding this world with joyful sonnets, lost inhibitions
beyond earthly scents and fragrances, combinations
Delicious and new discovered fruits of the vine
freshly distilled for lively, raucous, tasty libations
Expressions of universal joy, human perfection

A Magnificent Day   by Patricia LeBon Herb

a rainbow tie-dye bandana
draped around her head
not a stitch of hair
on her silk white body
she drives back
from the grocery store
diminished in size
her big blue eyes
look out to rows of trees
houses with fresh cut lawns
horses graze behind the fence
a female cardinal
on a telephone wire
a dusty rolling road ahead
oh, what a magnificent —
magnificent day.

rain invented showers

plumbers constructed
shower stalls
so we'd not see each other
naked
unless touching bodies in intimacy
   Thank you, showerhead, shower hose,
faucets
   make temperatures rise
   fall,
   on the beaches or in our homes
pipes carry water spray
   where wanted, needed
a million/billion items and choices more
   Thank you plumbers all
Thank you, firefighters, for knowing how to stall
   fire blazes, burning crosses and buildings, Teslas

Lovest all the children

Toddlers be the lovingest
   imparting fleetingest O-O's X-X's
   hugs measured, treasured most
At times withheld from strangers andst
   we grandparents always wants to hug tighter
Whilst we can grab them we askest for morest
   but once older they shyest
   awayest from showy displays of affectionals
Oh how I wishest my thirty-year-old
   wouldst hugest me the longest!
'Twas Love for mom ere she was a Mom, and
   love for dad, ere he was a Dad
   that didst make children purest
To grow, develop and live the longest
   with traits and characters, multi-abilities
   stronger than we couldst ever adorest
Let's lovest all the children

This is Living   by Charlene Brown

as this, another year ticks down last days
even though the sky is covered in gray
      though promises of next year may seem
filled with forecasts of rain
full of unknown twists, turns, dead ends
      though this year wasn't all you'd hoped
find joy anyway, in what was, what will be

one canary yellow flower peered out
      from between concrete wall and asphalt
all the breezes that cooled summer-bared shoulders
each moment of bright-eyed laughter
every single delicious bite washed through you
a stranger who let you turn into traffic
smiles unasked for, held doors
little victories in-between defeats
favorite songs, giraffe clouds, hugs, star-dark walks

this is fulfillment friend,
          this is living

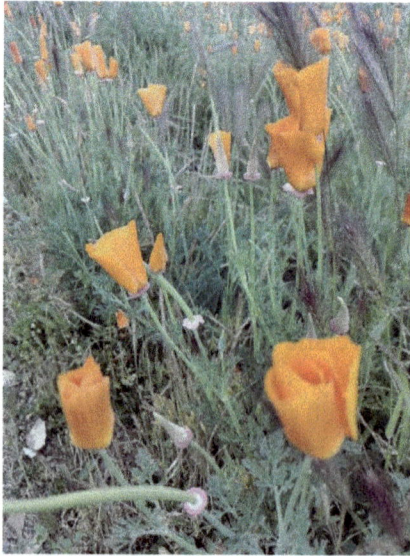

our better natures

free of sin, no human faults, frailties, knees skinned
to bind us to nature's corporeal existence
souls grow strong as do windswept plains in spring
as rapid rivers roar and surge in winter snow

bears, lions, apes, wolves may attack our bodies
raccoons scare and trash us, sharks chomp wet legs
when get close, they seek flesh to bite, swallow
can smell blood 400 meters away in seawater shallows

nature simply exists, possesses not evil in itself
darkness also surrounds us, but our light kills it
we adhere to ancient wants, unlike the animals,
we're greedy for gold, narcissistic rule, power

in vaunted airs breathed called maniacal
actions fill with abuses, cruelties undeniable
animals do not post signs for hunters of ownership
get angry, lust, envy, hate, nor seek revenge

blameworthy qualities, untold violent sins
when emanate from twisted homo sapiens
do not be ashamed. not a flaw. Overcome
life's supreme divine/human test, don't fall

forgiveness comes when evils of self put to rest
under six feet of solid rock packed earth
not to rise from their tomb-thrones again
lover's love earned through goodly grace

the kindness, justice, virtues you possess
override hateful inclinations. be an adult
in this spirit world which you and I partake
more real than darker animal instincts

human angels love, joke, laugh more
than any other earthly creature, even hyena
thanks to our intelligence and faculties of
meditation, reflection, and giving nature

"To act like the beasts of the field is unworthy of man."
—Bahá'u'lláh, *Gleanings CIX*

What Is Your Dream ?   Anonymous FB contact

Who are you?
What are your aims?
Your goals?

Maybe you want to do
a different task,
so, why do you feel shy?

Move forward
You are a hero
a devil never

Feel not hopeless
a hero always wins
You are the hope and dreams
of someone

Focus on your goals
Live for others
You are a legend
Work on your dreams

On the vernal equinox

the world comes alive
icy and barren trees and bushes begin to bear buds
leaves, stalks, flowers, or fruit.
grass grows greener, taller
hibernating animals explore outside
insects burrowed underground hatch from eggs
emerge to the surface, crawl, walk or fly
clouds which send down precious rain, revive
musk-scented breezes blow life-giving zephyrs
air is temperate, sun shines, fecundating wind wafts
through skies, clouds, the breath of life thrives
appears in plants, animals, homo sapiens, the world renews

"Earthly beings pass from one condition to another." said Abdu'l-Baha. As do I, we, he, she, they, them, you

Norman Rockwell hangs in my basement

A man like few others from the artist's golden age
he resides with me above my writing page
his print of twenty faces dressed in worldly garbs
speaks to me daily as raise my head in homage

There above me to the side, his painted cover from
Saturday Evening Post called The Golden Rule mosaic
speaks to all of the age we reside in:
Do unto others as you would have them do unto you

In gold letters to match the hearts of those depicted
like you, me, him, from foreign lands and home
all one family when carry their magic forward into
ever-advancing, ever-enhancing civilizations

Oh Frabjalicious Day! we have time left to say
out loud *happy thoughts and pleasing dreams come true
here as it is in heaven,* he said to do
when love each other, life goes ahead not back

home from work

laugh, cry, moan, groan, smile, guffaw
   Which shall it be when take on the morn
muddle through today's tasks and chores
   At work, serious breaks for long smokes
coffee to make me hot inside, keep mental fires inflamed
   Home, hugs from our child when walk in the door
releases love for my offspring not found before
  How was your day? from spouse generates a conversation
ask sincerely about her chores and obligations
   Soon a moment of grace, dinner cooked so well,
evenings fill with Scrabble, Clue, TV, and game shows
   All in all, **HOME SWEET HOME**
my private Green Acre, appreciate the blessing
   or could have been another dark day in Gaza or
   Ukraine, or violent protest, an anywhere civil war
it's all too sad for words, makes me mad, incensed

Why not, Christmas?   By Jenna Ayoub

Why not make a time capsule of
Christmas past and present
Or the sounds of bells ringing and
the smells of peppermint
And cocoa in a bottle?

Keep the memories of those we loved
and still do
Rekindle the spirits of the magic of
Christmas all year round…
With the hope and cheer and happiness and
celebrations of Christmas in our hearts.

What's the cheer all about?   (A Beautiful Noise)
by Jenna Ayoub

A curmudgeon would gruffly demand:
"Hey what's all the cheer about?"

To have a reason to be cheerful and happy

And grateful even
when it seems difficult
to do so

To uplift someone in
their time of need

Or laugh along with friends and family

And to receive a hug
from friends or loved
ones. This is the
meaning of the hearty
cheer felt and seen By
all those around.

Who you talkin' to?

You talkin' to me?
  Why you sayin' I should hate
his skin color or way she speaks
the clothes they wear on South Street
Who cares where "they" from, anyway?

You tellin' me? Let me tell ya
  Don't say those things, actions taken matter
Are they kind, sweet, helpful, generous?
Do they go outta their way to
fix my flat tire, deliver our mail,
fill my 'scriptions, laugh, smile?

What's that you think? I'll turn away
from decent folk like that
'cause you got prejudice
learnt from your daddy's daddy
without education, or livin' in a modern world
  Let's me tell you a thing or two

I been at Tijuana's border, inside Canada, on
Highway 101, up, down the East Coast Corridor
drove, ate, pissed, rode across ten states twice
flew through lightning storms, rode Greyhound busses
met super-friendly folks every which place
in London, Rome, Athens, Tel Aviv hangouts
Needles, Amarillo, Cincinnati, Chicago
just kind plain folk I tells ya, just
like me but not like you though

No, go off with those who share your views
stay close to 'em, rattle up your conspiracies
maybe's they'll listen with sad, closed minds
  I won't,
not one damn minute more
  Begone Evil Whisperer!
Take joy in magnificent diversity

What, Anyway   by Charlene Brown

A deer bounds across paved road,
invisible to dusk on the shoulder
stops mid-stride to stare, wild-eyed.
A distant birdcall warns of danger.
What, anyway, is fear?

A bruised mother leaves on a dark midnight
to drunken snores, carries laundry basket,
holds a wide-eyed toddler's hand
prays, begs silently for smooth quiet.
What, anyway, is courage?

Moss hugs a roughly scarred tree limb
in summer heat and winter snow.
Though dry-cracked or supple soft,
changes colors with time, never lets go.
What, anyway, is love?

Cuckoos wait and swoop in to lay
in another's nest; never build their own.
Depend on surrogacy, adoption,
fly away to get their own supper.
What, anyway, is selflessness?

Colors splash themselves over sky
in sunrise, sunset, light after storm
see them on display when flowers bloom
or in a hurried rush of salmon over stones.
What, anyway, is joy?

Fire consumes a forest with walled heat
races from ancient giant to sapling
indiscriminate, rushes on to devour
until only charcoal-ash scars remain.
What, anyway, is passion?

A vacant cabin, decades empty
settles into a softened hillside.
rafter, floorboard, waits until each year
passes it into camouflaged nothingness.
What, anyway, is peace?

Today gonna be happy!

Oh yeah, invited to sit down traditional
Christmas dinner by sister-in-law & hubby
two awesome but sickly kinfolk I pray for
In their kitchen it'll be wine and toasts
salad, roast beef, and scalloped potatoes
baked and topped in melted cheddar

Oh no, a call, canceled, host ill and crying
Ease her sadness, say *No problem*
Oh well, alone with my bedridden wife
It must be for the best says good ole' St. Nick

A text from my sister, *come over for dinner*
Gadzooks! Christmas not lost, a feast
with blood family, even brother from Sweden
Yes, yes, some jokes, good food, comradery
like our old weekly Pasta Nights at huge round table
Rush right over, politely pig out, chat loud

Whoa! Get a text from brother's wife
that doll he married, the second beauty in line
a son of their own, so chiseled, tall, two more
we adore all five of them, good people to know
their spirits jovial, party givers up with L'Chaim
Now her parents inviting me for turkey at 5!

They knew I'd be alone
How awfully sweet of them
to think of my at home singularity
but still full of sister's festal board from 3
Thank you, Santa, for granting my wish
too bad my poor wife can't swallow leftovers

Can't bring home turkey, ham,
crisp golden stuffing, even overcooked soft pasta
won't fit down her inch wide PEG tube tonite
unless it's tasteless Kate Farms liquid
delighted though, she's still able to stomach it

Love all ways

"…the first bestowal to the world of humanity is happiness, that kind of happiness which is unalterable and ideal.

"If, by happiness physical enjoyment of material things is meant then the ferocious wolf is made happy because he kills the innocent lamb and satisfies his hunger for a few hours, this is not happiness."

'Abdu'l-Bahá

"O ye beloved of God! Know ye, verily, that the happiness of mankind lieth in the unity and the harmony of the human race, and that spiritual and material developments are conditioned upon love and amity among all men."

'Abdu'l-Bahá, *Selections from the Writings of 'Abdu'l-Bahá*

The nine-pointed star symbolizes the highest unity. Its points signify the highest digit, major religions and more

The Majesty That Is   by Sarfraz Ahmed

Don't blink
Don't think
Don't say a word
Let the moment evolve you
Revolve you
Dissolve you
Until there is nothing left
But the memory of you and I
The sun, green sea, blue sky
The magic that surrounds you
Close your eyes for a moment
Get lost in the view
The majesty that is
Me and you

The most said words in America

I've got to… or I will…
I love you…
Please… or Don't… or Stop…
It won't happen again.
Seen any good movies?
How about those [enter sports team name]?
Did you see… or know… or hear…?
Oh My God!
I would like…
Thank you.
Praise the Lord and pass the ketchup.
I promise…
Whatever you say, hon.
I will lower taxes.
I want your vote.
Do you love me? (show it)
Of course, too, unfortunately, FU

Dream on   by Graham Blueskies

Sitting by the window at the desk within my office,
attempting poetic lines sipping my cup of promise.
It's not going well today but I know the reason why,
I'm sad wanting another's note, so I let time go by.

Thoughts whirlpool like revealing nothing new,
each one ends with loving thoughts of you.
A heart has no defence its centre clearly exposed,
gets pumped to the point it can only explode.

Hope you know the words you'll be saying to me.
Might make tears,
                    might make joy,
                                    could make both you see.

Are we meant to be broken to reach out for a fixer?
Are words just token from a wicked baseless trickster?
My heart's burned, soul bared, loaned to you,
feeling futures will soon be bound, as one not two?

You looked picked me at my midnight hour,
set me in your crown a cherished special flower.
All further struggle pointless ever vain,
to rescue each other would be our only aim.

Still at my desk cloud gazing through windows
Wondering.
                    how far love's words
                                    cast a dreamy shadow.

The Store Card

Prime by Amazon
online shoppers' topmost choice
Noon delivery

She's our girl

Sweet as a cup of
   Twinings lavender tea, warms
      hearts on wintry cold days
Smarter than a woodland fox
   in the ways of living with others
      who treasure her friendship
Adept social butterfly since age three
   enhanced high school Key Club as secretary,
      scored field hockey goal victories
Hardworking, reliable and dedicated, a
   loyal and devoted employee
      turned self-made candlemaker
She's a daughter who makes us
   proud to be called parents, graceful gemstone
      on the diadem of humanity
A superwoman despite vertigo disease
   lights up every heart and room
      with words of encouragement and ease
An accomplished talent, bright
   wed to a fine Irish architect
      of red adventurous beard and moustache
Motherly as the best and kindest, she
   shows her toddler son propensities needed
      to grow strong, loving, intelligent
Their future, safe, whichever place it may be
   a cliché perhaps, may they live in peace
      Wherever Love is, she will find them

incredible

- how strong Saturday sanitation workers are
whom I used to call garbagemen to my public dismay
- New York Times delivery at dawn since '79
- voice, app, or mouse click and its delivered today
- dial tone steady when pick up the phone
- sandwiches, coffee, anything at all, ready at the window
- Chipotle's hands to my mouth in five minutes
- Your love these past five decades, even more reliable

Letter by Letter   by LACE

Grandma your fingers
formed the words
letter by letter
your voice could not emit

Our time together
scheduled by your cancer
The twirl of your fingers
in front of your face
your smile emerging
blue eyes shining

"You are my beautiful girl"
I saw you say

You felt the vibrations
of my tears
hundreds of miles
apart

In type set
your words came
by mail

In each black
Letter by letter
I saw you heard me

One summer you came,
pointed to my piano
I refused, covered my ears
to be like you

You sat me down
I played the notes
You kept beat on the frame

OH! The music we made

Stopping my hands
letter by letter
you spoke with yours:

"With my fingers I speak,
with your fingers
you will sing"

On heaven's perch
you rest
on our bench
I remain

Grandma
note by note
my fingers sing

In them
I hear you

I found the wind
       and fire
       in   you
you found
something
you loved
in me too
       cosmic mystery
       love's conundrum
       made real
       over ganga for two

when young we experimented
then got older together
children born; mountains hurdled
I can never repay you

Gotta Love HP

as creatures go, men are literal, lineal,
one thought, one step, one task a time
not like computers or women who bend it
to their will, never slow, tasks done in tandem

human time measured in days, months, years
computer clocks slice millisecond meters.
plodders like me, slow as molasses but
wife's ministrations like my PC, instantaneous

functions of programming and algebraic codes
computers multi-purpose, multi-mode.
we're built of blood, flesh, sinew, bone,
execute in bits, bites what we can, alone

PCs have cameras for eyes, sound cards for ears,
speakers for tongues, jpeg or png photos
internet apps galore, some I despise, others adore
amazing AI software runs thousands freeform

we human AIs however, all agree
at times accurate or otherwise downright bizarre.
each of us deficient if perfection required
still, love my PC for correctly spelling
the wrong answers

   /A+ Dunkin coffee \
/XOXOXOXOXOXOXOXO\
\it's not just the liquid warmth/
\i prefer the light roast beans/
 \at 5 every morning no lie/
 \drive 3 mi, smile wide/
  \knowing it's open/
   \ready to put on/
   \my card a large/
    \just for me/
    \XOXOXO/

Middle Age Woman   by Charlene Brown

We aren't twenty anymore, or even thirty
our tummies aren't taught,
faces edged with laugh lines
and whether covered or not
there are gray hairs that catch the sun

The dresses we wear have pockets
flowy skirts that skim over the right places
shoes now comfortable over showy
we break into off key lyrics from
all the times when we
danced, drank, and darted across streets
carefree and looking for love

There is light in our eyes
we love blue skies,
charcoal storm clouds, vivid sunrise
see peace in autumn and forgiveness in rain
we hold wisdom in our hands, try to blow it
like kisses into the hearts of our sons and daughters
hope they notice, catch it from where it hangs in air

Future

One instant from now
unforeseen
being shaped
Mine too, unfolds, molded
by yet unknown, unforeseen forces
when the living but not yet real
meet
Life! So exciting this way!

brother Chaz

tree climbin' man extra careful, extra wise
father of three good sons like Robert Young
operator of turbo-charged Mustang for fun
cookout party organizer, toastmaster roaster
do anything for you kinda guy
almost died from a blot clot to the leg
at 17 years younger than I
feared the worse, has decades left to run, enjoy
life with equally stunning wife Dawn.
close buds with friendly ex, kids happy betwixt
thanks to him, yes, Chaz the Jazz man
plays uplifting music as party host,
for the whole rootin' tootin' clan
tellin' jokes, sharin' laughs, holdin' hands,
gives each cheek kisses, gaily wrapped presents
at birthdays and holidays like Christmas
New Year's under mistletoe, Ayyam-i-Ha specials
this hard-working honcho the best friend
a brother ever had
like yours

what is love, a novice asks

not for me to know how Cupid's arrow flies
how it strikes, what an ageless anomaly it is
from romantic history pages past
so unexpected, or a love secretly expectant

how do I tell my son about sex
what intimate details should I share
he'd know I'm revealing his saintly mother
who's not a female but his Venus ideal

do I tell him my exploits with L.A. women
when love was free for a toke or just the helluvit
or couch it literary like Wuthering Heights
what does love got to with it when only fifteen

She Sets Me Free   by Sarfraz Ahmed

The cocktail sun pours all over me
In waves of emotions
She caresses and undresses me
Bathes me in the deep blue sea

Scrapes away my troubles
Peels away the pain
Heals this wounded heart
Torn apart again and again

Consumed by sadness
The dark clouds
That once circled me
In waves of emotions
She baptises me

Reborn in beauty
Reborn in love
She sets me free.

ONE

The Tao that can be told … not the eternal Tao.
The name that can be named… not the eternal name.
The nameless… both Alpha and Omega.
The named… the mother of all creation.
Ever desireless… one sees the mystery.
Ever desiring… one sees signs, manifestations…
Every wise one says: *Myriad paths to truth exist.*
I've crawled, walked, climbed fifty-six to mine.
You may have one or hundreds in your Valley of Search.
Best wishes for what you find.
It won't be found in your wheelhouse

The Comfort   by Sarfraz Ahmed

We all seek comfort in the familiar
In things that hold us
Remind us
Capture and bind us
In memories long-ago forgotten
In things that mean so much
So precious and pure
Memories kept hidden and secure

Taken out in times of comfort
To blanket us
To cover us
To protect us
A fortress built to contain us
From the hurt that the world has to offer
You long for strong arms
To wrap themselves around you
So you don't have to suffer

My dream is…

to love my fellow man
A high bar to meet
admit I'm beat
when try to love tyrants

Doesn't seem right
to love someone
cruel to innocents,
who's a narcissist

People can turn a new leaf
I pray that happens
before I…
        disembowel them

Hummingbird   by Jenna Ayoub

It's not a moment too soon
That I write these words
To lift you up.
To express the thoughts
Pondering upon my mind and heart
And like a beautifully colored
Ruby hummingbird whose wings
Flit ever so slightly
Demonstrating its striking nimble
Flight of fancy and shimmering body
I sometimes feel suspended in air too
By the wings you are giving me.
I admire the ruby-colored hummingbird
Whose heart beats as quick as a beat, too fast.

Said my Noon Day Prayer

Like a million other obligations
  hard to remember
  unless spirit's memory tickles me
Electrical current similar too
  sparks when goes ungrounded
No places to go tonight
  like human teenage touches
Unless find the right
  lover both fun, intelligent
Charli and Nolan
  found each other at Dunkin'
When casually mentioned
  A pair made in heaven
  Why don't you investigate

heart flutters by elliot m rubin

it's early evening,
randomly, i met her
a few months ago,
now, she's boarding the train
with a one-way ticket
to deep in my heart,
when i finally decide
to leave my old baggage
on the station platform
and begin over
with a fresh start
to go to where
i always wanted

with no return ticket

Mirror, Mirror, for the Ball

Turn you this way and that, jaunty or flat
Look green with French mustache, sage beret cap
Try the Cowboy look in tall Stetson hat
Don black bowler from English milliner

Which should I choose to complete this costume?
Want an impression when enter ballroom
Pass through crowd, avoid masque of blood red doom
Partygoers dance, drop dead under moon

Stone abbey's nave a place to hide in sack
But the red masque spy's my grey hair dyed black
Undoes its facial cover, *Oh, Blondi!*
Looks like the new Broadway star this eve
    Spared masque's deadly touch, not her prey.
    Watch *The Bachelor* in comfort of chalet

*In memory of Edgar Allen Poe and Shakespeare

Touch Heaven   by Sarfraz Ahmed

Sometimes find myself
Going back to summers of my youth
Long hot summer days
When whisked away
To sandy beaches
We'd touch heaven
Feel the sun upon our backs
I remember the smiles and laughter

I want to go back to all these places
Want to experience it all again
I want to ride the waves
Feel high tide rush in
To touch heaven
With you by my side

Traverse the expanse of space

Speed through heaven, pierce inky nothing
keep open longing, searching, inner eye
Look for what you dearly hope may spy
set down your ship, stop bemoaning Earth's demise

Myriad gems and diamonds buried in stars
pry out golden nuggets from behind ironclad bars
Fold, meld, implant pregnant seeds onto new planets
Earth once barren too until rain and wind began it

It knew you would come back, find yourself again
the prodigal son, lost but the returning heteronym
You were gone, now the happiest feeling found
amidst an ordered universe of fertile ground

Too few words of gratitude means
couldn't say enough for such a life well spent
Will others recount them when we die?
Let's hope for the best

Beach antics   by Graham Blueskies

An iron cauldron cradled above the open fire,
a soft red sunset in its last throes, watches,
 waves lap languidly, hypnotically,
along the almost deserted seashore.
Cool night airs carried softly by the breeze,
on other business paid them no heed.

Tongues, no longer talking conveyed urgent messages,
hands explored eagerly as breaths came ever more rapidly,
hearts raced as they chased, searched new landscapes,
like bursting fireworks, burning with bright intensity,
 crackled, faded, fell silently back to earth,
resting sweetly, trusting in each other's arms.

Marriage Institution

Anticipation, expectation, excite this convocation
Promises engraved in gold bands for certification
    part of this heart-planned ceremony designation
Commitment and future bound in resignation
    to the will of God and trust in no abnegation
We two vow hearts, minds, souls in mutual subjugation
    one to act for the other, no surprise revelation
In sickness, health, poverty, or wealth declaration
    this day a momentous calendar commemoration
The implication tremendous, without decimation
    portents of sophistication without cessation
Honeymoon vacation follows prolonged probation
    but what's in store have no inclination
Will experience unexpected severe tribulation
    but unification strong, no serious perturbation
The presumption by all is joyful procreation
    activation proclaimed by progeny's promotion
Our solidification endured from this unambiguous quotation,
    "Marry, O people, that from you may appear
he that will remember Me amongst My servants."
        —Bahá'u'lláh, The Most Holy Book

eyes of love   by elliot m rubin

she had them
both alluring and irresistible
falling in love was easy
those brown orbs
had a way of signaling
without words
her intentions
yet i knew
what they said
what they wanted
and somehow

what i desired

20 not 5

we should know what SSSTT stands for
those overtaxed senses we abuse incessantly
what our complex bodies experience, simplified
so small-minded, infantile, circumscribed
to think the good Lord only gave us five

we also balance on tightropes, know where we stand
in space, alter cell chemistry in our bodies or in minds
and thoughts, we sense movement and ghosts,
time passing too, sense degrees of cold and heat
imagine pain or feel relief, and mostly, the spirit's touch—
without which we'd experience none

only spirit reaches the unsmelled, unseen,
untouched, unheard, untasted human soul every moment
yet we develop it not, nay, don't hasten it along
we let the charlatans explain it, tell us what to believe,
how to perceive it…
indeed, if smart,
discover for yourself what it means to be alive

Shoulder Your Burden by Roberta Batorsky

It's not yours to shrug off.

Our solar system's sun,
with resignation,
abandons
mission and position.
And, once rested,
begins a new day
doesn't need convincing.

Shoulder your burden
given the grace you were born to.
Overturn insincerity,
decry falsehood
repel force with persuasion
and the knowledge gained
over a lifetime.

Earth's magnetic force
exerts its strength
to protect us
from strong solar winds
without inducement.

Shoulder your burden
defy pretense
bring conviction and belief
to what you do.

Accept the struggle,
resist platitudes
with truth and persistence.
Bring along wit and empathy
for good measure
to light your way.

Went fishing at Stony Brook

This Rocky Hill spot of Uncle Jack's, quiet
   picked me up, handed me his extra rod
Let me hook the worm, cast into the pond
   we stood and chatted for a lazy hour
He cracked me up with crazy stories
   what boy pals do in fumbling teenage glory
Here I was, now his favorite crony
   he ten years my senior,
      horny as a night owl
Later at age fourteen learned what girls liked
   didn't let randy classmate's raunchy tales
      discolor gentle entrances to heaven

for the love of Pete

or Mike, Daniel, Willy, Mehdad, Dion, Ivan,
or any man, it starts with an attraction, just
like a man feels for a woman, or younger
girl for girl, boy for girl, girls crazy for boys,
what age can anyone swear
that true love is real

high school sweethearts marry, so do seniors,
divorcees, widows, two, three times when
love pierces the human breast, eyes, heart, limbs and loins,
hope springs eternal like Alex Pope said

Who among you can say this magic love
only comes from one place
Must it be one way or send us to jail
We all account for our misdeeds upstairs
no need to legislate our hopes to death

Love-filled or love-starved human hearts
it's a private matter is it not
Don't dare legislate love

Laugh with surprise

"Oh, peoples and nations!
Arise and work and be happy!
Gather together under the tent of the unity of mankind!"

—from *Paris Talks,* 'Abdul-Bahá

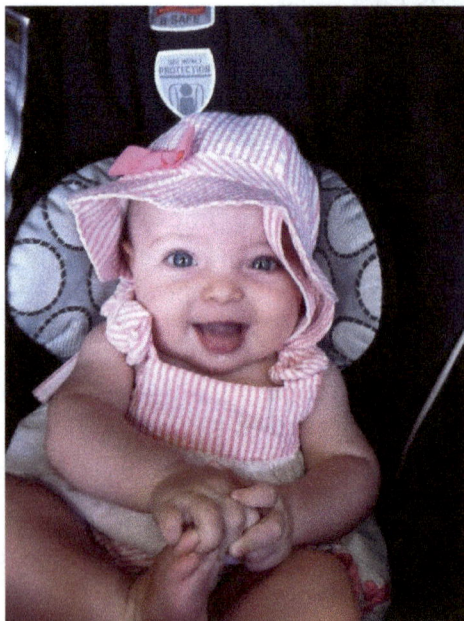

Joy winds

blow hard, fast, over low, high alike
as they always have, no pause, no respite
never stopping, not for a nanosecond
    blow spirit into body, soul, you
    bestow love, perennial happiness

they don't create sorrow, hurt or cry
sobs of pain have no power here
when winds of joy caress your face
your tiny naked body exults in breath
from the instant your soul joins in
to the instant your soul leaves for
kingdoms of Wonder and Gladness
indescribable, unimaginable
rewards for a kindly reputation

for now is the only place
    with you
    here by me
    free to love
    every creature

he made this planet ours to enjoy
no end to pleasures since birthed
in that tiny body we each once had
nourished, loved, grown, adored
in a corporeal incubator of potential
our spirit-self calls… me

at least etch "Thank you"
on your tombstone in gratitude
for his word of genesis, "Be"
the rest, dear friend, is becoming

Fat Cat Sat On The Mat   by Karuna Mistry

Fat cat who sat
sat on the mat

Fat cat who ran
ran into my flat

Fat cat chased rat
life to the max

Fat cat grabbed
tore my woolly hat

Fat cat who shat
shat in my shack

Fat cat attacked
my veg patch

Fat cat and a bat
chased with my bat

Fat cat who sat
sat on my doormat

Fat cat, furious, how I spat
spat at the bloody cat
(and that was the end of that)

Fat cat – just a cat
please don't call the bureaucrats
(I'm a dog lover really)

My Dog And Your Cat   by Kauna Mistry

Outside my dog sat
Sat and slowly he had shat
My joys of collecting his crap
Discretely in a small plastic bag
What must my dog think of that?

My dog saw your cat
Saw where she was sat
Said to myself, "Oh crap"
As he darted across quite fast
I know he will not let go of that

My dog chased your cat
All the way around the flat
Your cat is lean; my hound is fat
Sorry, but I could not help but laugh
At the sight of seeing the silliness in that

About my dog and your cat
I categorically did not know that
She was an award-winning acrobat
So when my dog came round your flat
She showed off – I give you credit for that

Whilst my dog and your cat
Could never conceive to begat
I was hoping we could have a chat
Tell me, what do you think about that
Or should I also chase you round your flat?

Neighbourly   by Karuna Mistry

Hi, can I have a quick chat? Your cat just shat in my back!

Your garden back?

Yeah, I think you'd better do something about that...

What do you want me to do – nail her door flap?!

Obviously, something better than that...

Okay... in my truck, I have a baseball bat...

Great! I could swing with that! #Whack!# Owww!! Why did you do that?!

Well, I just did 'something' about that...

Hmph! My turn – now here's my slap! #Smack!#

...I have a better aim than that!

Now your cat has scatt-

-You'd better do the same – scat!

That's not a bad idea, that... I'll get my *own* baseball bat...

Are you thinking of hurting my cat...?

Well, control your cat, or face my attack!

Curb your anger, else you'll have me *shit your back!*

The Cheese

A rat in a maze
Sensing, smelling, closing in
Knowing it's
within reach
Aware of itself?
Instinct
Not wasting time
Detours and dead ends
remembered
Two persons inside
one soul
one rat
Both merge in Love's tasty embrace…
Muenster

is it not a fact

we love to laugh
at every jot and tittle uttered in jest,
pun, funny word, bar joke or blonde jab
laugh
when things dire or bleak
release pent-up tensions
crack a smile, smile a crack
not think back of worst to come
only grim realization
we've had our chance to
serve at the net
volley back, forth, back
win the match
on our own merits, wits
abilities, character and strength

that's a good laugh too
we all got help from someone

Ferris Wheel or Ferris Buehler

Legends in their own minds
both odd first names not often seen
One rides around, up, around again, down
overlooks pretty sights of circuses and towns.
The other sings Top Notes of *Twist and Shout*
after Wayne's original *Danke Shoen* gets 'em riled

The oldest one in Vienna stands taller than
two hundred thirteen, love cab bulbs lit up.
The younger one, five-foot-seven and a half
cajoles Cameron his neurotic best bud
to extract bitchin' Sloane, his girlfriend, to
ditch Glenbrook High, crash Chicago's parade

What fun to ogle milling crowds below
from gondolas in London's Eye high and above.
Joy and laughter flows as the school chums
outwit their hardass dean, Mr. Rooney
who hails a school bus as his car is towed
dog-bitten, pants ripped, split-lip, muddy

Minds of their own these Ferris wheelers
dealers, stealers, feelers, roundabout keelers.
Watch them spin up, up, down, down
not stopping for mice, men nor clown.
spin till leprechaun Ferris shares their pot of gold
What would I give to be one of them!

American Express

Dread the blue name on the envelope
your blue-lined statement enclosed
Good though, excellent
keeping tabs on charges I owe
How else would I know
what my love bought weeks ago
when I wasn't looking

A Unique Magical Dream by Deepti Shakya

I was on a dream trip beyond the galaxies,
A surprising journey full of mysteries.
I was mesmerized by the shimmering stardust's canopy,
Charismatic sounds echoed like a symphony.

Suddenly my eyes fell on a rainbow glittering like gold,
Countless magical things beyond imagination to behold.
Stars twinkling like diamonds smiled widely, happily,
A rare fascinating dream beyond reality.

The grandeur of this magic astounded me,
Such wonderful fluorescence filled my heart with glee.
I couldn't believe my eyes that I saw this dream,
When I woke up, I was surprised with a scream.

Sometimes dreams show us things we can't imagine,
It was unique and bright, true, just like the opaline.

What if they were

California girls in deep blue bikinis
match ocean's color with piercing azure eyes
blonde straight hair blowing as lag on by
wishing boyish dreams into reality as their
rollerblades offer the kindest female charity—
a smile at you with a Mona Lisa wink

they exude peace, lightness, fun and surf
in every curve and line, from long leg to pinky
Hand to shoulders, neck to sky
here to wish you happiness and joy so fine
on rollerblades of Playboy promiscuity

What if they were white doves not blackhawks
in every nation, land, and island high
Instruments of war abolished, guns destroyed
What if we felt safe to live our lives
on rollerblades of promised love like that

the picture in my soul

eyes can spy a dim candle's flame
twenty miles away in a mountain niche
why can't you see
my fatal flaws
correct them before I stomp your heart

my ears hear birds warble, sing and lark
outside on spring and summer afternoons
why don't they unlock
my envious heart
to be happy, free to fly as they

my nose inhales the fragrance of your perfume
as we undress to consummate our vows once more
why can't I open up
chat with candor, a light demeanor
instead, hold feelings of envy apart

our throats whisper *I love you* together in bed,
times spent on physical sharing but no secrets
why aren't you
in my heart every second I live
to remind me I'll love your face forever

lotus

knew zilch how to crunch numbers
in the new job conferred by chance
boss depended on me so tried your math
on spreadsheets of business finance

the standard at the time throughout
common big or little organizations
required putting digits in rectangular boxes
deleting rows, columns, or adding functions

taught by the seat of my pants, had
no instructions or hand holding mentor
by trial and error and lucky providence
our gyrations together proved hard evidence

The great sirocco of happiness

Blows across meadows, flowers, plants, trees
Its waves crest over rivers, lakes, oceans, seas
Winds snakelike across valleys, mountains and vales
refreshes insects, animals, man, woman, child
Brings peace in sure knowledge to unsure America
Nothing need be sad unless a Chimerica

Every moment on our clock has purpose
How welcome when hands turn to joy
our mistakes forgiven, corrected, forgotten
make love, give hugs, truth to our namesake
Forsake hurts and hatreds for future's sake, gone

Join hands, arms, grip shoulders tight
walk in serried lines and proclaim
this Day we live in is the greatest
civilization of humankind ever made

Love stands ready to end these ruinous wars
Cooperate, be each other's helpmate
Smile, laugh, tell jokes every hour
let's watch movies in the den together
marvel how science fiction came to flower

We are the blockbuster of our own making
the director who never slows the action
always filming in place, whether Hollywood or Texas
We, actors and actresses both, our roles to play
make every frame a happy beginning foray

Not sad, not dour, not bad, nor sour
After all, tonite is Earth's Happy Hour!
where the rowdy come hang out and play
on a planet made as pure as heaven

all we must do, be the lump of leaven
kick out the trash, make the streets safer
have sex between true love's silk sheets
call a never-ending ceasefire to weapons

donut heaven   by elliot m rubin

i didn't realize the opportunity
a donut shop would have for me
until i tried a chocolate crème
a filled round one with dark chocolate
overwhelming the top, as my taste buds
exploded in orgasmic ecstasy
the franchise booklet looked delicious
my salivary glands sealed the deal
i bought the shop and set it up
donut heaven for non-diabetics
every flavor on display behind glass
where skinny folks grow their juicy fat ass
cinnamon holes and powdered sugar
vanilla cream or chocolate-filled
if you eat one, remember
i sell it fresh and hot
buy a donut or a dozen lot
leave your diet at the door
eat one and you'll want more

Banish Glossophobia

#1 on everyone's list of fears, #2 is dying
We're all nervous when we think about that

The solution, simple, open your mouth
    Exercise jaw, lips, tongue, larynx
Put aside anxiety, unstick the words in your pharanx

Plenty of hacks to get you prepared
    Remember the audience wants to like you
Just visualize them with no clothes on
    not yourself standing before them naked and bare

Jersey boy

most of my life, but born in D.C. the non-state
didn't matter, hometown northerly Trent's manor
like the core of Mafia from Sicily's Palermo
migrated wherever easy money took me
followed Brucie, Frankie, Nancy and brother
Queenie, Connie, Whitney, Bon Jovi too
we all know the Hoboken lingo
like *How's ya doin', Joe*
no need for o u or letter g
we completely comprehend
drink wudder by the gallon, liquor too
get in fights, toughened by
Catholic priests, Sisters of Mercy
who wore black belts and swung rulers
not garters, to stop spitballs flyin' outta windows

there's a special place in heaven's hell
a corner with a three-legged stool
just for us Jersey kids who were made.
when reach the promised goal
hope to fix the Golden Rule
over a nice dish of pasta in gravy
at Sal DeForte's Italian ristorante
on Roebling Av in the Burg
come and join the family
made right here in America

I went to Philadelphia once…

but it was closed.
Contrary to what W. C. Fields said
to Mae West in so droll a tone
always found it fun and open
but laugh to think it aloud
The way he drawled it out
had to be there, I guess
He's awfully funny for a man
too many others serious, stoic, dull

Sweetness   by Graham Blueskies

It's true what they say
about sweetness…
   only lasts a while
like candy on tongues

it melts without trace,
taste sits long in memory…
   something we chase.
I want to sit with you

while away hours to
share my eyes…
   and my soul.
Let's take in stars as we stare

out to space,
forget hate filled words…
   in this world.
It's true what they say

about showers.
They only last for a while…
   like walks with you
in the park or the fields,

they reveal more
in the few words…
   we conceal.
I want to lay with you

in the dark for hours
bear witness to your hopes…
   and dreams.
Let's trace out our scars

as we stare into space,
feel as one in each moment…
   we taste. Make memories
one day we will chase.

hate pretentious names by Rodney C. Richards Jr.

like mine, the full one sounds just odd
middle initial and junior suffix detract from
Mr. Rogers neighborly manner as everyman
shorter it holds more promise like did Rod
Taylor, action hero in Herbert George's *Time Machine*
or, Rod Serling—genius, writer, producer
fans fav his unworldly *Twilight Zone* series.
converted from Rodman Edward later to
The Outer Limits, sometimes feel like that
in left field, or Burgess Meredith alone in the vault
hundreds of books on dozens of shelves
he toddles out to find his city rubble reduced.
so happy he is! can read until heart's content
but breaks his glasses on concrete cement, Alas
then I feel beaten like Mr. King by LAPD
a life of joy destroyed by cellphone video   But wait!
Rod Stewart sings songs so sexy sweet
feel like renaissance man meant to bequeath
a name sans pock-marked face, recorded for history

mystery solved

2 pm at the big Post Office
one that anthrax shut down in 2-0-0-1
after sickening 22 who all the locals knew.
minding my business, drop letters in blue box
flashback to a card I once held
remembered from my dear Psychiatrist.
Crap, late, speed up the highway asphalt
past cars, through lights, park, climb stairs
rush up to counter, apologize, Russ looks
   No appointment on the books
What?! Scratch head, another delusion?
make an appointment on the spot.
at home find the card, sure 'nough
clear as ink black blood, it says *today at 2*
the doc filled it out, not her assistant
no wonder she forgot, must be bipolar too

Living Together

loved her before said I do, love like
Romeo's teenage heartthrobs for Juliet
after fifty years of legalized union.
she's my go to emergency contact
on living wills, HIPAA forms, POAs

resigned through experiences together
do not win catfights or arguments against her
she knows everything since day one
when kissed her at the summer dance
she listened polite to my nervous teen gibberish

lists of likeable things about her abound
often overshadowed by hard demands
placed on my shoulders, in my hands
in my gut hourly, whether shopping, meds, chore
tasks must be done with immediate assurance

our unspoken foundation, love
care for her above every earthly vicissitude
as much as she does me, tall order from
the get-go, fulfilled in kind when watch
two severe illnesses eat out her insides

not the chores so much, as hoping
to please this helpmate who chose this interloper
caressed me, consoled me, saved me
from dead-poor decisions more than stars shine
through Earth's cosmic atmosphere plasma

out of love and respect, know she
wants what's normal, expected
couldn't be happier she picked me
will enjoy fewer years we have left
until, our bodies spent, both lie in rest
next to next

be the tornado   by elliot m rubin

gather your winds
unleash the fury within
don't hold back
let the world know you
face the ignoble
ignore the ignorable
the lemons of society
sour happiness for others
blow past the passable
rule your life to its fullest
enjoy society's sweet, sugary
watermelons
they wait for you to cut through
to devour tasty fruits of life
know deep down in your heart
when the angel of death visits
you will have ridden the wind
with your chin up
          and no regrets

only two sure things

say every sage, wise man, guru, messenger
Death and Taxes guaranteed
come high or short order, hell or deep water
wage taxes on paychecks, sin and luxuries
property, home, healthcare to Feds, State, municipalities
sales tax on every purchase, even groceries, antacid
social security too although retired ten years ago
income from all sources tax levied
investment dividends also, IRAs and capital gains
let me rocket off to heaven alone, at least
a $255 SSA check back for my white pine casket

a match made...

five hours of Saturnalia fifteen years ago
white tents and canopies, dance floors of teak
lively music whistling strong through the yard
friends greeted the couple, relatives cheered.
two hearts grown dear within two years

i wanted to walk my son up the winding aisle between
occupied chairs, white-cloth tables covered
in wreaths of fresh-cut fauna, flowers arranged
by his sister's happy hands in celebration.
wanted to hug our first son once more, wanted to say

I love you more now, as a man of honor
one final time before lost him to his bride to be, an
off-Boadway actress talent who sang from Huppah's stage
of long-stemmed tulips, in adoration a sonnet to serve,
obey, a prayer for intertwined destinies

co-workers choo-chooed down from the City, found
coffee brewed, noon teas to satisfy, long buffet,
three-tier marzipan yellow cake filled plates
gave looks of merriment tasting purple flowers
homemade by old and faithful friend, as

scan our empty yard now and its garden labyrinth
visions of them wax nostalgic, strong as that noontime promise
to bind their powerful marriage and new daughter,
a bounce to our hearts in every smile, her dreams matter
a child of the universe born into happiness because

faithful to each other, they brave tempest storms
climb hills, bury hurts, inure to hardship, making
history as lovers cemented over coffee
in Piccolo's Village store many years before
their connubial touches, kisses, spirits still endure

the machine

There once worked a scientist in Washington D.C.
invented a time-bending device in 1963
After JFK shot, he turned back the clock
the great President served for 5 years more
America salvaged and his Camelot restored
But Congressmen heard of it, carted time off
guaranteed their reelections, only few scoffed
With no term limits, America easily sunk
what you get from stinky political _____

trip your Light Fantastic

reach your inner self, flick the switch,
a light bulb fills the empty space
visions of unity begin their race
not for us to wonder how
rays that streak out
dispel shadows, remove doubt

a new world where peace reigns
people love each other like
their very own mother
not a dream, switches exist
to make ourselves shining lamps
flashlights that persist

we have batteries and the Grid,
our own hearts, minds and wishes
don't think love can never happen again
look how founders established justice
in 1776 and 1787 discussions.
we'll have a much stronger constitution
when add an Equal Rights Amendment

Be joyful

"I want you to be happy… to laugh, smile and rejoice in order that others may be made happy by you."
—'Abdu'l-Bahá

We ♥ our customers

Children, youth, adults, seniors
  matters not what age you were
As long as you purchased a fine thing
  from my store
you are friend for life

Your dollars keep me in business
  for sure
Help me grow to a giant conglomerate
  boost my ratings
Shares on facebook, yelp, amazon all help

I could not have ten employees
  if not for you
One day it will be thousands
when my S&P, Dow Jones,
  and Nasdaq scores
investments on the leaderboard

I ♥♥♥ you
this is true
The international colors of your
  cash, coins, checks, credit cards
keep me in the black not red
Thank you for being loyal

Visa   Discover Mastercard AMEX

Really owned by the banks you know
JP Morgan Chase, Citi, Wells, BoA, PNC
Goldman runs the show, tells the government what to do
After all, America runs on credit and debt, not Dunkin'…
although, the bubble hasn't burst yet

Just That   by Patricia LeBon Herb

I want to spoon
with you

right here
right now

under moonlight
on summer grass

hold you close
hold you dear

no talking
no kissing

just listening
just that

I want to spoon
with you

under moonlight
on summer grass

hold you close
hold you dear

no talking
no kissing

just listening
just that

Burning Haibun

The Lord and the Taylor strolled over to AMC Paramount Theatre on Broadway and bought front row tickets to see Amazon's new James Bond in *Tomorrow Never Dies Again* studio cut for the press. Expectant (it had all been hush hush), wondering who will play Ian's ageless spy protagonist this time

…Lord and Taylor   bought   tickets   Expectant   all   hush hush wondering who will play   Ian's   spy protagonist   this time

The Lord   hush   will play   protagonist

the saints come marching in

it was a lawless town named Dodge
saloon, hotel, barber, bank on Main
stable at one end for visitors and ranchers
fights and killings over cards and whiskey
buried with no glory in pauper's graves

the territory became a western state
times a'changin' no mistake
a stranger rode in with silver badge
said his name was Wyatt, they all laughed
he soon introduced his gun-totin' brothers

it was rough for a while, establishing law
until one day a gang of outlaw cutthroats
challenged the boys at the O.K. Corral
citizens scattered but Wyatt prevailed
they buried that gang without a trial

more sheriffs spread out, and deputies too
towns were safer, people and children grew
judges were hired and juries selected
fairness and common sense spread like Covid
with angels of justice throughout the land

ya couldn't ask

for a better wife
home
 job
  car
   career
kids
 friends
  even relatives
no loud neighbors
 to make her delicate sleep worsen

the income enough
 some left over after bills
  dinners out
       at Wendy's, Dairy Queen, Macs drive-thrus
sit downs at Longhorn for steak tar tar
    until she could not bear the travel chair

enough to rent cable and streaming RSS feeds
    furnish the house attractively
use two computers, two iPhones for texting
an iPad, Kindle, and whiteboard to write
Alexa to sound out audio tunes, four TVs
NIX for scrolling past family photos every day
    and remind us how lucky we are, were
          until cancer and ALS combined
          struck you down in your older prime

the question always arises
why do the good ones die
 What did she do to deserve this?

yet she is free of such a burden
 doesn't moan or gripe or blame
  had a great life, good spirits remain
happy, oh so happy, smiling, laughing
  when grandkids come to visit, play
    while she looks on from bed, clapping

The Sirocco of Life

Blows
as it always has, will
no pause, no surcease
never stopping, not for a nanosecond
It blows
Love, life, perennial happiness

Don't make it the cause of sorrow.
hurts, cries, and sobs of pain won't stay,
remember the wind of life caressed your face
on your once tiny naked body
the miracle instant your soul joined it

With you free to love your maker, and
everyone you see, even strangers
he's made this place an endless playground
pleasures to be savored since you were born
in that tiny body of ounces and pounds
grown, taught, nourished, adorned
in this corporeal incubator
we call physical existence, home

Until the instant your soul leaves this Garden
for the Kingdom of Wonder and Gladness,
where indescribable joy, wealth, health
reward the living for good lives spent
here on Earth, in a place and nation setting
for the temporary breaths we're granted

At the least, guaranteed
we'll etch "thank you" on the tombstone
erected in your honor
if you were kind and sublime
before your untimely demise

I just ask

Never hurts to ask
Will never hurt you
unless you beg
for a punch in your gut
Some answers are like that
flat out *No* for example
does that, you should know the answer first

Mistakes are like that too
When order coffee on the go
a little cream, sugar and
when I get home
open the lid
   It's black
I hate that
too lazy to drive back
Add milk, sweetener
can't tell the difference
Just another something
to bitch to friends and neighbors

Life is bucketfuls of No's and disappointments
Not one of us perfect
I know that
still ask anyway
Expect a *Yes*, expect the right order
maybe shouldn't be so gullible
after all, like everyone says
Life's a hot chick on roller skates
and we ain't in the Rollerdome no mor'

So just say *Thank you*
when the girl on roller skates comes by
take what you can honestly get
Build up the courage
ask her name
That works best

How to be happy, based on (good) science

Express gratitude! enjoy fratitude, sistertude
find certitude in the love of God's creation,
in men, women, youth, children especially
  Be social! what the hell, people are interesting!
  Act happy! forget your blues and troubles
  Increase novelty, excitement, when something new
  Differentiate your taste buds in your human loves
  Help others, after all, more angels will help you
  Exercise a little, walking does the job just fine
  Sleep well and dream. Oh, how better it will be!
  Spend time in nature—in the park, take a hike,
    snowboard down a hill, sing loudly, have a lark
  Be honest and kind when you tell the truth,
    you don't want your soul ebony black
    no matter the color of your skinned head

How to send happiness away

  Be a stick in the mud, ya know?
  Be negative all the time;
    and have no friends
  Do more of the things you don't like,
      like that no-fun job with only regret to show for it,
      and a piss-poor pension for you and your wife
  Bemoans, groans, and sorrow will turn your life
  Continue 8-hour smartphone and social media use
      emails too, waste time scrolling picture screens
      meant for one purpose: sell things and make cash
      for somebody else
  Don't say "Hi, how ya doin'?" to neighbors & strangers
  Don't hold open doors for shoppers
      or pick up trash under your feet
  Be a curmudgeon. But advice to the wise in you
      join Ebenezer on Christmas Eve
      experience Past, Present, Future before you're stuck

  Parts above gleaned from *The Washington Post* online 12.22.24 with
permission to share, personal views added

rub your magic lamp

the world and sky turn inky blue/black
like Mick sang his paeony of grief to
doors painted black and mate's hearse
drove back along the cemetery blacktop

but man and woman too smart for night
invented light from fire to shine from glass
seen to cover earth from outer space
where every moon inspires a lover's might

our greatest gift, intuition and intelligence
sheds light where shadows and darkness dwell
on words typed here or afloat in my head
but my lifelong companion, sadly owns
a knife-sharp brain with tongue of lead

fan the flames for me
within thy wise brave breast
let loose thy dreams of sights unseen
rub twice this magic lamp where genies dwell
never live in fear of life's demise

remember always there is light
at every tunnel's end
no matter the darkest dreaded
or how difficult to lift thine head

What's fair game to a writer

Novelists have it easy, they blame their characters
for upsetting mores and readers, they don't worry
Memoirists, the tougher lot, reveal secrets in dirty laundry
name names, behaviors, that run courtroom risks of libel
Journalists, if good, follow Edward R's rules, else lie
Poets have it best, it's fair game to us, can bare souls and eyes
we share jabs or jests, lean right, left, or down the middle

Original Songs   submitted by Jeanette Bergeron

Below are two songs that my dad, Edward J. Wilson, 1932-1995, wrote that I had memorized. He was a Philadelphia Police officer for a year. He left to attend the seminary, only for a year, because the GI bill wouldn't pay for religious education. Hence, the subject matter. His bipolar disorder was pretty severe. He couldn't hold a job long and finally got disability benefits when I was 10. Nevertheless, he was gregarious and loved by neighbors and almost everyone he met. These songs are among my fondest memories of him and made us kids happy!

Policeman Song   by Edward J. Wilson

I was standing on the corner,
not doing any harm
Along came a policeman,
who grabbed me by the arm

He took me to a little red box,
and rang a little red bell
Along came the wagon,
to take me to my cell

I woke up in the morning,
and looked upon the wall
Bedbugs and roaches having
a righteous game of ball

The score was 19-20;
the bedbugs were ahead
Until a roach hit a home run,
and knocked me out of bed!

In jail they give you coffee,
in jail they give you tea,
In jail they give you everything,
except that doggone key!

Sunday School Song   by Edward J. Wilson

Young folks, old folks, everybody come
Come to Sunday School and have a lot of fun
Please check your chewing gum and razors at the door
We'll tell you bible stories you never heard before.

God made Satan; Satan made sin
God made a hot place to put Satan in
Satan didn't like it, said he wouldn't stay
He's been a little devil ever since that day!

Chorus

Daniel was a wise man, the wisest in the land
The King didn't like it, said he wouldn't stand
He put Daniel in a dungeon, lions underneath
But Daniel was a dentist and pulled the lion's teeth!

Chorus

Samson was a strong man, strongest in the land
He could lift anything that dynamite can
He leaned against a pillar and the temple fell
Everybody in the temple ran like hell

Chorus

Along came Noah, stumbling in the dark
Picked up an axe, built himself an ark
Along came the animal kings, two by two
The king Jackrabbit and the king kangaroo

Chorus

(Add your own!)

Raise a joyful noise, but not that joyful

The Word is, the Lord rose, but we missed him
Descended on clouds of confusion, misinterpretation
Leaders tried to fool us, said they knew the path to heaven
Jonestown the worst, so too Rancho Santa Fe and Waco
When false wolves lead, use your heart and intelligence
Swallow pride, adjust your goggles, run far far away
Rose-colored glasses easy to find

The world of giving

From all our people to all of yours
 here to wish you happy days ahead
filled with family celebrations
 brunches of hot buttered English muffins,
dinners of thin linguini and seven fishes
 meatballs smothered in marinara fixins'

We hail from sunny climes or steamy jungles
 ice caps or snow-white sandy beaches
mountains tall, Mt. Massive, Denali, Whitney, Rainier
 islands Catalina, Jekyll and Wolf, Silver Dollar
aged forests Redwood, Green Mountain and Sierra
 covering vast historical expanses of roamers
lifting by bootstraps adventurous American dreamers

We enjoy drives in our SUVs to campfires
 morn, noon, and night under crescent moons
with names Copernicus and Seas of Hope
 Showers, Tranquility, Fertility, and Acceptance
Next day we meet again, join hands with our clan
 brothers, sisters, aunts, uncles, cousins
nieces, nephews, parents, grands
 we guileless children... smile, hug in glee
Tales overflow of hijinks or millennial peace
 at our backyard Fourth of July picnics

Celebrate and stay with us the week
 our Sestercentennial soon upon us
if we make it in one piece
 but don't feed the richest 1 percent the most
Don't settle for table scraps after taxes taken
 living here is better, though, the best most avow
 than others who hope they had what we do
Admit it, even our poverty surpasses plenty
 it's why we stand taller, freer, better
when donate to DEI and worthy causes

happiness in 1931 and 2025

Volstead Act, the rule between two oceans
passed in a moody phase of alcoholic guilt
by American Roarin' Thirties politicians
hounded by Christian axe of Carrie Nation

speakeasies, gangs, bribery, corruption
all them shoot 'em ups inside Chicago limits
police far from honest, crooked hungry judges
served crime boss bastard Al Capone
used baseball bats across the head
on those who didn't condone him

it took incorruptible agent Eliot Ness
to bring his cronies, underlings, to justice
bustin', breakin', their breweries, speakeasies
workin' outside of Cappy's cowed police
who turned, walked, looked the other way

De Niro played the heavyset Al, sent to
Alcatraz for tax evasion, not murder
not mayhem, nor fear, nor robbery or liquor
only stopped when raked in 2 million illegally

he went to federal prison for crimes untold
signs of mental illness readily apparent
brought on by syphilis in his loins, mind
incurable, it could not be bribed
unredeemable, he screamed, died

so it shall be to every criminal enterprise
when Lady Justice finds you
the queen of fairness and equity
makes it stronger for the rule of law
to govern all, we pray
even those with powerful riches

The Fall of the House of Usher II

A story by the master Gothic novelist
    how shall we compare its 1839 venue
A long time passed, surely, we've changed
    found better spirits within us
Built stronger mansions, exorcised demons
    solved problems plaguing us decades, maybe
No question this house haunted by irascible devils
    wars, injustice, starvation, displacement, pestilence
On grand scales we've replaced ideals with pragmatism
    calculate cash pros and cons of social programs
If you've been affected, infected, rejected, dejected
    not much to be done except admit
This House of Cards lamentably defective
    not joined by wise and moderate mortar or cement
We entertain ourselves though, have gadget screens
    Internet access, and LEV vehicles to whisk us off
Family, spouse, children, congregations aid too
    when government abandons its share of duties
If all else fails, call county and municipal angels
    health services also care for poor families
No need to feel alone, sorrowful or destitute
    Man's plans may not save you, but his will

Bumper sticker questions

Do I judge the driver a fool for supporting
a candidate I think is awful?
Or are they wise when turn out all right
and vote to keep my Social Security afloat?
That truck with the big flag waving
what does it really mean to them?
A patriot despite what ills must be changed,
or a diehard supporter of life, liberty and freedom?
Rather, my automatic brother or sister
because so am I

Women, Women, Women

if you want a perfect and balanced world
you can call livable, fair, not severed
despite that in the Garden we took a fall
consider a strong woman, reliable, unself-centered
walk side by side to show she's treasured.
accept her vow to stand by for eternity
no way she would trash me or be mean-spirited
as long as faithful, upholds my unspoken warranty:
loves me completely even when beleaguered
makes me safe, secure, top priority
may turn topsy-turvy or nag if displeasured
but knows as one together, we can't be untethered

*partial ballade inspired by Yoko Ono's song Men, Men, Men

the problem with teeth

we break out of gums around age 1
by 2 got 'em all except wisdoms
which 4 often take out much later
like when mine hurt so much so crowded
ate pizza when home from dentist's chair

a sad tale once tartar buildup ferocious
cleanings 3 times a year not enough
bad lower molars only left one to munch
implants didn't take cause addicted smoker
saved by root canal and crown, thank goodness

that's just it, brush and floss religious-like
or pay the ultimate price, denture paste
but must have gums for them to glue to
so heed this piper, brush often, chew thorough
worry later about Crest whitener

Cry Out

Cry out O Lionhearted
from on top of Zion
Cry out to your Lord
from on top of the world
Circle 'round in adoration
gather up your courage
Cry out O Lionhearted!
Lift up your voices
no longer shy

- Adapted from the song Queen of Carmel

Peace in our lifetime

Peace brings happy-ness
to you and to me, every-body
It will come, you will see
Violence will vanish, banish-ed
like threatening storm clouds they are
One day soon they won't apply
hearts will mend
as quick as the doctor can
suture an open wound, salve a sore
Trust the divine physician
who knows the disease
listens closer than your life vein
prescribes correct medicine

If love were extinguished

The power of attraction would flee
Affinity of human hearts
dispersed, ceased, disappeared
Light would succumb to shadow
Darkness, hatred, bloodshed prevail
Sight would be obscured
Hearing, touch, smell blocked, shut off
Music in souls would spit out dirges
Flights of fancy crash and burn
To what is left of earth
No one would find joy, mirth
Joy wouldn't be remembered
Life would cry out *Oh my! Why!*
Can't hide our life, keep love locked up tighter
than army's gold in a Fort Knox cellar
Love must let loose like two seas
join them and merge eternally
give hearing to the deaf, sight to blind eyes
Magic will return to every ill or thirsty soul
music, dance, joy lives on each moving beat
We'll rejoice forever because love greater than hate

it looked bleak

fires, wars, chaos created hell on earth,
in hearts, in closed and siloed minds
they wanted control of what they shouldn't have.
along came a man made of water and lightening
beclouded in storms of rain and electric flashes
he never paused nor stopped nor hesitated,
turned fire's violent flames into holy spirits
people, buildings, rivers, mountains capitulated

good people had prayed hard
for scores of thousands of years
yet stumped to solve the Gordion riddle
how regain God's trust and peace on earth
like Eden before the poison apple bitten
how expel the serpent of flesh and materialism
remove havoc, fear, death to innocents

a council convened at the Palace of Hague
where peace once formed after horrible world war
representatives spoke their hearts
bared their hurts, begged for justice
listeners paid mind, cried and sobbed along

then the Aquarius man spoke into the mic
You are on the path,
    unity the only way to establish oneness
Rely on scriptures and knowledge,
    science, fellowship and IT, but
    one thing governs above the rest
Open everyone's hearts
    with unbounded love,
    shake hands and sign a Pact
If don't do this,
    expect darker chaos and
    greater injustice
    to run rampant, unchecked.
Lasting peace will never appear

Chameleons

Hidden toxins infuse air and water
    daily cancers spread gore into patients
radiation's glow, chemo injections
    cause side effect sicknesses, ugly bedsores
Chameleon chemicals hold relief
    if you can spot them first but
won't be able to, not alone, not yourself
    You'll need a doctor's prescription
Green pill for no envy, pink for empathy
Blue for uppers in legal quantities
Red for sorry, orange for in-between
Lily-white for Take your Pick
Yellow for pain better than aspirin
Black with codeine in the mix
Brown for murky *Hope this helps*
"Release me" from pain each tv ad promises
    to child, teen, adult and ailing senior
But an insurance card they require
    Look for the elusive White Rabbit
    in every druggist's Rx plastic bottle
Know in advance there's no sickness panacea
    to troubles which assail us, unless God-given
Thank goodness, plenty of them exist, and angels

gotta love doctors

never quick enuff—for an immediate appointment
    unless blessed to have a walk-in clinic next store
without health insurance, out of pocket grows large.
    so hard—the path for them too—undergrad first
pass MCATs, pay med school four years, finish
    residency in 3 to 7, pass licensing exams
then start practice from scratch—unless a specialty
    add 3 more for a fellowship—then magically learn
how to talk/listen to patients—diagnose correct cure
    we wait, dependent—heads full of migraines for sure
without psychiatric drugs to fix mental disorders
    which creep pervasive-like into the daily vernacular.
doctor, doctor—cure thyself if you have enuff money

Pashtun San'wich by Roberta Batorsky *For Rebecca*

Two footfalls past fences
the military base's landscape
abruptly changes,
revealing multitudes of humans
trudging in ceaseless,
ancient migration
on quiet, anxious lines
which file past tents
inflated to capacity
where vaccines await arms.

Dark eyes blink over masks and
flowy hijabs stir without wind.
Women and babes in
colors from another world
radiate pain and disruption
and no language suffices
to ease the transition
or relieve anguish.

What resolves: a blurry portrait,
reposing in shattered glass:
a Kandhari mother
missing her wounded husband,
steadies herself on my arm.

I offer a hungry toddler my san'wich.
Turning my back,
suddenly two more tiny girls
peck at it,
three fluttering,
hungry pigeons in the park.

My gratitude for being human
is boundless,
smeared between two slabs of bread.
My Pashtun san'wich offers a glimpse,
a taste of this precious connection.

things, things, things

the worst god-awful word invented
by Germans but had to be by someone
oh yes, it is, things, things, things
we use it for every "thing"
converted from ping
for "the appointed time"
always crosses my mind
sticks between my ears
inside my mind always, insistent
clawing, obnoxious, a pointed generality
do this thing, do that thing, now
this moment, can't wait an hour
or till I finish my Dinkin'
only later if lucky
tomorrow will be good enough
but it won't let me procrastinate for long
this word older than English
used for ages to mean any "thing" at all
whether serious or flippant, commanding
or demanding. "things" must get done
or the world will stop spinning
I'm sure

I love Don't

Don't you? be honest it's true
Who among us wouldn't say
Darling, don't worry about a thing
to a sickly son, daughter, or wife in bed or
a student who'll miss the Science Fair deadline
But you have a car accident, can't keep appointments
Don't be so hard on yourself
you tell a friend, assuring him his wife
loves him way too much to divorce him
over a drunken business trip dalliance
So, you add *Don't jump to conclusions*
But she kicks him out and files next day
Ya gotta love *Don't,* but use it sparingly

Embers Inside   by Charlene Brown

Wake, walk down stairs
light flickers, all switches off.

A log placed on fire too far dwindled
to light quickly and gift heat,

but it burns now. Flames lick the bark,
an old limb consumed from within.

Pass to the kitchen for water,
marvel at the persistence of embers.

2024 new Age

unspeakably glorious – he came like a thief
in the night - just like the prophets and Jesus foretold
at our wit's end, we knew not - how to abolish war
bombs, missiles - drones that obliterate
guns that murder – children's dreams and dolls

but God, exactly as promised - so damn often true
like times in yore - came through once more
sent the next - a rod of iron, tongue of fire
who'd lead us to peace - when awoke from slumber
when inhaled faithful fragrances – would bloom into life again

he did, roared upon waking – Earth shook with thunder
could no longer ignore storms – his times a changin' song
abolished hateful old tunes – *Let them go*, he said
released rock music – wrote new lyrics to sing
raised heroes, heroines - remarkable children

their bravery enough - to make all nations safe harbors
built permanent homes - broke Earth no more
streets rang with bells – jubilation not heard before
people gathered freely – around the happiest globe

some enchanted robbery

he knocks on the Colonial's door
companion in black stands near
two American pals wait inside van
with bated breath, expect no answer

Knock, knock, again, this time louder
Bang, insistent
aware of the plan to break and enter
    hears, *Hello? Who's there?*

taken aback, didn't expect response
must think quick on rubber-soled shoes or
the plan goes down the pneumatic tube
once a thing guaranteed

old knock knock joke surfaces
Um, Sam and Janet
    Sam and Janet who?
Sam and Janet evening, he belts out in tune

they run like hell, the van running too,
jump in, hot, stuffy with sweaty armpits
Cool Sammy Sam shifts into reverse
peels out, turns, rushes out of town

What the hell? Janet red hair says
The Tempts said no one would be home
Now how do we steal
the million-dollar diamonds?

Sam says, so cool
Have Plan B, of course, next time will answer
Noah.
    Noah who?
Noah surprises, Noah excuses
Open the door!

wherever you are

you can find peace like I do
sitting alone lazing
on a redwood bench
back against vinyl garage wall

hear the prop plane soar past above
lazy calm hawks circle overhead
watch robins strut and hunt for worms
observe neighbors, some wave, stroll by
enjoy this sunny hour march on

covid vestiges subsiding slowly
Israel's invasion longer than expected
yardwork begins in earnest next week
beef ravioli dinner the favorite tonight

no demands except what agreed to
paid the Feds their taxes on time
only something not right
can't quite put a finger on it

some families are sad, out of place
now deportees from this once free country
their pains, deprivations touch me
everywhere they didn't before

time gathers the young at heart,
smarter, fairer minds, philosophies
kick political party poopers out of town
leave America grand again
better than before

Hide me, Mister Sun, from you

must shield my body from your daylight rays
most powerful star illuminating the race
nine-three million miles away, you burned my face

first you struck my tender temples
doctor's scalpel bookmarked hazel-tinted eyes
felt quarter-wide scars on each sideburn side

next you burrowed into thick calf muscle
derma doctor did his up/down/sideways hustle
ugly crossed incisions look like Golgatha

then on skull a Kennedy half-dollar popped up
he scraped you off, hoped to end my dilemna
hair once there, gone like last night's supper

right forearm scab popped too, needed exorcising
a three-inch gash and slash necessitated, sadly
now a stark white scar mars once golden arm

you struck a rear wound on my head again
four hours later Mohs surgeon cleared its margins
thick black stitches, bleeding lasted weeks on end

then two big spots on forehead merged together
required scalping like wild west Indian's souvenir
size four by three inches. Not a tattoo I hold dear

your scourges can't be stopped, nor constant UV light
leaves my virgin skin little to smile about
so wear jaunty hats to hide disfigurations

color now matches unscathed feet at least
covered by mismatched dayglo socks 24/7
today, just heard, biopsy back, Mohs again

You Are All I Need   by Roberta Batorsky

Not knowing where love stops
or begins
I bury myself in you
for my hungering heart knows only
a hangdog winter.

I rush to you
with surfeit or loss
my emotions loosened
in your warming breast.

Neither art nor device
can lift this dread off me
You are all I need
to signal my new season
and nudge this frozen shell
back to life.

With you I am the hidden spring
or the shaded stalk
hesitantly blooming
where new growth stirs, shudders
and sprouts.

Sorrow yields to opportunity
to announce the looming spring
my love extends its righteous span
sighs, grows to overflow.

People are great

Give 'em half a chance;
peace, security their cake
Justice their icing

Beyond Galaxies   by Graham Blueskies

Share with me your wounds,
take a moment, let them surface,
it's safe to allow your fears,
to fall within my compass.

Here is something more,
something to rest your truth on,
unlike promises tacked on doors,
Shoulders made to cry on.

Let your hands be held,
be led gently, along the climb,
look deep within my eyes,
see love's easy to find.

Here your heart is cherished,
all cares, eased, ceased,
never trapped, yet secured,
to traverse life's Galaxies.

What are you searching for, friend?

A Wiki How to, or encyclopedia answer?
Amazon toy for grandson's 3rd birthday?
Software to keep nasty malware out?
Tickle Me Elmo from antiquity or Hess Truck
    from three Christmases ago? Try Etsy.
Scores and highlights on last night's ESPN?
How about great-grandfather's whereabouts in 1901?
    Send a saliva test to Ancestry.
Anything you want to know, or buy, or trade,
    available online or maybe Amazon.
On Google its 8.5 billion daily searches, daily I repeat,
    more than people on this planet pray for meat.
Did you find your soul yet? Or record your Voice?
Tell me when you do, and which URL, please.

Coffee Drinks

Dunkin before breakfast
hot sweet smooth joy
sip swallow gulp
its throaty taste
warms insides
want another

Spit out, choke, crunch
lukewarm round carafes
popular   overrated
frown at high cost
tall or grande
always bitter
Starbucks*

* Light Roast saved them

Cry out, O Zion!

Have seen the coming of the Lord
　　the mountain saw and felt it too
　　but the rest played deaf, blind, dumb
He came to bring change
　　the likes of which never seen
Too bad no one wants the status quo to go
　　unless it fattens their wallets
　　or removes their woes
Only shadow men and women angels
　　glimmer what's in store
But it's never been a secret
　　the forces of eternity
　　unleashed ultimate glory decades ago
Blessed to live in interesting times!
　　as part of the human race

I Acknowledge

we've gone through rough times
You and I, still enduring one now I see
whether sickness or disease
ruin or displacement
we've all lost someone dear

I cry along with your pain

when sick, I hoped to get well
fired from work, bounced back
banished from home, survived
but dad's funeral triggered hospital stays
knew him only two years before he died

sadly we all lose loved ones

the world can be a shitty novel
but love, joy, recovery, possible
in fairy tale hopes and as we troop on
not willing to let our spirit die, or call it quits
despite faceless doctors itching to pull the switch

they know not what they do, he said, so true

let minor victories give you comfort until
that day when the world holds us like babes again
in that hour, every minute will not be a fight
to enjoy a simple long held breath
along the gamut we run to gain eternal life

it's a long, hard race. had enough?

until the end, love unconditionally
grab the final peace never known before
time to let your spirit soar
roam through all the worlds in store
promised before mommy's tummy grew large

She's happy when...

I'm in her bedroom suite
Tell her I'm going out, why
Text when I'll be home
Once back, listen, hug her, she cries
Remember it's her birthday and
never forget a card like I once did
Respond immediately to her medical alerts
drop what I'm doing, go to her side, administrate meds
Remember she's in bed and cannot move
Treat her like a human being, not an invalid
Consult with her about spending our money
Value her opinion, directions, decisions, points of view
Remember her mind still sharper than mine

She's happy when I...
Tell her I Love her
Remain to watch TV together as she expects
Won't send her to a nursing home, promised
let her pass peacefully in bed as she desires
Pay property taxes and bills on time
as she used to do like a Turbo Tax fanatic
Enjoy her company watching *Elsbeth* and
Only Murders in the Building which
make her smile since she can't part her lips
Forget she's lost her voice; interpret her pointing finger

She's happy when she...
Doesn't have to excuse her mistake and
say *I'm sick, I can't help it*
Happiest when the kids and grandkids visit
they cheer her heart so much she cries happy
tears to have them in her weak arms and hands
Makes it through another month with ALS
breathes in, out, her slowly closing chest
lungs sinking lower, lower in her hospital bed
    We're both happy in the morning, when...
    I open the door and her eyes aren't shut

could speak a long diatribe

a manifesto against myriad ills overdue,
imperfections of sick people, leaders, but
to what avail, you know that already
feel powerless to intercede
in our position, just poor souls are we
trying to eck out dimes from dollars
pay taxes, rent, raise families
so close our eyes, let others deal with it
until tornadoes wipe our house away
rains pour, turn roads to raging rivers
fires burn forests, cities, towns, stores
or some buzzsaw swinger fires me from work
and so on, and so on...
rather, praise those who get it right
first responders in every catastrophe
vaccines to chase down demons
FEMA, Red Cross, church ministries come to everyone's aid
judges adjudicate law, not party partisans
education bans ignorance, prejudice, not books
God's messengers show the path, follow them

My dream every night

hauntingly clear, so real kick covers off
wake up sweating
Lady Justice has disappeared, gone
nowhere to be found
insanity, exploitation, mental illness prevail
killing and shootings for no reason
like that ungodly movie *The Purge*
is that what it takes
to wake people up
from eyepatch-covered sleep
closed ears, minds, hearts, spirits
as too many scream *Give me mine!*
I hope, pray, cry out
Life is greatest without a doubt
when love all humankind

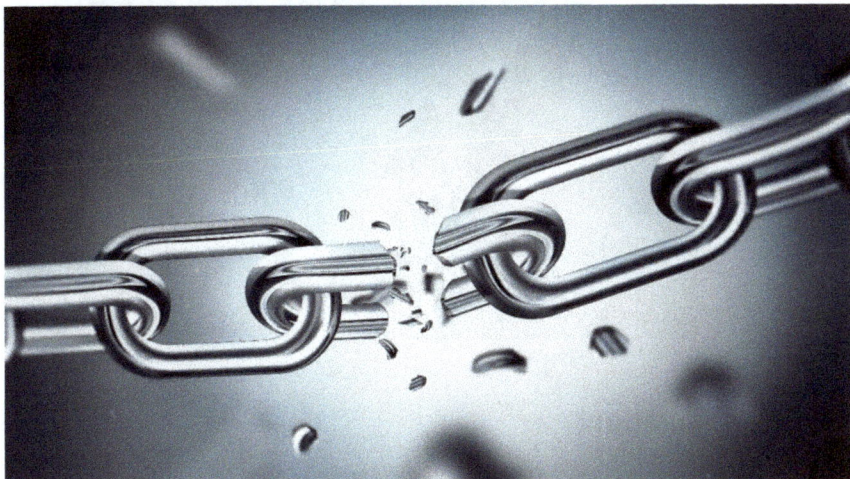

Speak

Break your chains asunder
give voice to what is right
to overcome might
Don't let fear make you hide,
for freedom and truth
truly worth the fight
Real joy and happiness come
when shine a light
on dark shadows
Then deport hell's bad politicians *
back to Hades sound bites
and jail enclosed corners

* Not to say all are bad. Hard to agree 100% with all views of politicians. Those who do the most can be commendable.

you were an angel

conceived in dreams of parents' thrusts
not nearly an act to forget
regardless of circumstance
you are pure, a benefit
some forget
you can propel yourself anywhere
the angel inside forever exists

does not the babe succumb to the child
the child to youth
the youth to man or woman
yet the child is never gone
nor youth
nor man, nor woman
nor angel

Epilogue

You'd make us all happy if
you outlawed weapons*
bombs
landlines
missiles
ICBMs
MAD
AMDs

and just plain stopped…
this madness
hatred
fear
distrust
disunity

we'd save a helluva lot of money
and lives
pain
suffering
tears
nations, nations!
heal our broken hearts

*But kept proper weapons to quell domestic violence, catch
criminals, legally hunt, defend against attack, and obliterate any
nation that invades another.

America, you don't own me

although born in your District of Columbia
in shame, not a state yet
I am a child of Earth
world citizen par excellence
worked for your companies legally and
as public servant handled your money
upheld your laws as they changed
to suit the times as needed
and boy, did they
like your Constitution and Amendments

the closest our race has come
for billions inhabiting this shared place
the Declaration of Human Rights
with judiciary to apply and make interpretations
legislature to ensure access and fair treatment
funding for social programs not political
executive to enforce, promote, what's right
PSAs, public radio, balanced news media
uphold freedoms, be fair and guarded in speech

America, you don't own me
a citizen of this world while alive
every state should raise three flags
theirs, the nation's
the world's
and follow ideals
not implode or choke to death
from greed, lies, false promises

uphold your principals
be the best republic possible
enhance federalism
keep power in the hands of your people
faith in the one we trust
not his image on the Almighty dollar

the end of my whining

so tough, impossible to stay neutral
world affairs are everything
I mean e v e r y t h i n g
political bents and ramifications

groups hate each other for past hurts
what happened a hundred years ago or five
make demands today, this very moment
nations distrust the other's every lie

treaties and promises broken
while the planet heats up, storms, fires, seas rise,
rain, mudslides, earthquakes, volcanoes, tsunamis
special interests ensure they're satisfied

you have a plan I believe
know what's best for humankind
always have and they were told it
ignored it, drowned themselves in distractions

so hard, unbearably hard, to stay neutral
ride the middle, moderate, waning wave
believe your plan better than man's
whether takes one day or a thousand years

until we're sure
we can trust ourselves, others
shake hands and hold arms
agree and make it better
to live free in peace
in time

I run with the don-o-van

not in a black white segregated van
but rather a dayglo-coated
ken kesey boatmobile arabic camel caravan
with red poppy floppy flowers all can smell
attached to front/rear baby boomer buggy bumpers
—joy on four wide racing firestone tires
with fat white letters screaming
Peace! Love! American Graffiti!

not entering a devilish hell
but on our way to ganga heaven
where whiskered walruses play sitars all day
into evening YMCA campfire songs
like John Paul George Ringo did
for a year in Jimmy's Margaritaville
or was it the Maharishi bending their ears?

until all of us flew home to Liverpool
to find our secret garden of
transcendental meditation for 75 quid
where octopus's squid live
under blue-green seas of bitchin'
meter Rita mermaids
surrounded by happy tunes and lyrics

etched into mood rings
sold by you and me
singing Hari Krishna
proudly displayed on both pinkies and
good 'ole Betsy Ross USA flags
flyin' from Ford pickups
so never forget where we started from
running with don-a-van
in circles of requited love

It's a new beginning

It's time you wake up and smell the roses.
—Anonymous, everyone

Wake up, get up, do something.
—Anonymous

Gotta get up and try, try, try
—Pink song, *Try*

Be assured of our heartfelt prayers in the Holy Shrines that
Bahá'u'lláh may bless and confirm your endeavors to realize, to
the fullest, the extraordinary opportunities of these precious days.
—The Universal House of Justice, *Turning Point*

Guest Contributors

I'd like to thank my friends and fellow poets who submitted a contribution to this book. Many I've known for years on weekly Zoom critiques, others are new. All are devoted to the craft and expression presented by poetry, and I applaud them.

Patricia LeBon Herb is a poet and painter who currently lives in Middlebury, VT. Her poems have been featured in *Vision and Verse* (ed. Les Bernstein 2024)*, Phases* (Redwood Writers 2023 Poetry Anthology), *Zig Zag Lit Mag*, *Borders in Globalization Review*, and the Swedish literary magazine *Provins*. Patricia is of Belgian-Native American descent. www.lebonherbart.com

Karuna Mistry is a British writer of Indian ethnicity. He released his debut poetry book, "Sojourn: Transcending Seasons" (2024) via Amazon worldwide. To date, he has over 80 individual poems published in more than 50 anthologies. Karuna is poetry editor for Austur magazine.
Instagram / Facebook:
@karunamistrypoetry
Web: **karunacreations.wordpress.com**

Sarfraz Ahmed is an Amazon bestseller writer from the UK, who achieved success globally as a poet. His recent work includes *Pardon Me…You're Stepping on a Poet* and *The Ramblings of a Romantic Poet* (2023). In November 2024, he was nominated for a Pushcart Prize for his poem 'Uncoil Me.'

Deepti Shakya hails from Uttar Pradesh, India. She's completed three years Engineering Diploma in Computer Science & Engineering, an AMIE degree in Computer Science & Engineering, a bachelor's degree in English Literature & Sociology, and six months Certificate Course in Web Designing.

She is a Bilingual Poetess, an Artist, and Reiki Master Healer, and writes poems in both English and Hindi languages. She has been awarded Global Poet 2022, Alexander Pushkin - W.B. Yeats International Literary Award 2022, Poet De Pride 2022, The Christmas Literary Honors 2023, Sparkling Soul Award 2024, The Poet of Nature Award 2024, and Global Poet 2024.

Jeanette Bergeron is a proud wife and mother to two grown daughters in the arts. She uses her time in retirement from public service in health care policy and regulation to practice and support organic gardening and farms. She also volunteers and engages in civic and Bahái activities and community building. Jeanette serves on the Green Team for the Environmental Advisory Commission in her hometown.

LACE is a Central Jersey native who writes short stories, essays and poems while pursuing the completion of a degree in Art History with courses in ASL. The greatest positive influence in her life was her deaf-mute grandmother, the inspiration behind this submission. An avid photographer and small business promoter, her work can be found at vangirlwrites.com

Jenna Ayoub, whose first name is Jennifer, has always wanted to publish poetry of her own and stories of her own as well since she was five years old. Now 42 years old, she has had award-winning essays published in a competition when she was in high school and college. She has also been a college intern for a suburban newspaper.

She plans to publish her first book this year. These are her most recent poems published.

Roberta Batorsky is a poet, science journalist and college educator. She's written poetry for about 5 years and is in several online and in-person poetry and fiction writing groups. She is also putting a book of her poems together. She's been published in Fine-Lines and Heron Clan and has been a freelance reviewer of Life Sciences textbooks.

Her science blog is https://solipsistssoiree.blogspot.com + RobertaBatorsky_poetry (Instagram)

Charlene Brown lives in the foothills of Yosemite, where she teaches English, cooks, hikes, and enjoys her years as a mom to three. She is interested in how nature and life intersect, and explores themes of family, justice, and society in her poems.

She can be found on Instagram under the handle **poetallyb** and is looking forward to publishing her first collection of poetry soon.

She likes to photograph nature around her too, here below:

Graham Blueskies was born and raised in the Staffordshire town of Wolverhampton, made a city in 2000 by the late Queen Elizabeth II. He left school at 15, worked in a department store, but spent most of his sales career in the engineering sectors. In 1982 he married, then moved to a village near York with their two children, which they still enjoy immensely.

After an enforced early retirement, his focus returned to writing, charity fundraisers and volunteering. With the help of friends, he has also written and recorded a few songs, the most notable being 'My Street,' used to raise funds for the homeless. He enjoys long village walks. A brief venture into UK politics saw him stand as a candidate in the 2005 general election. Graham was also an amateur DJ for a community radio station and at other fundraising events.

"I may have retired from work, but I have not retired from life."

elliot m. rubin is a best-selling New Jersey poet who has published over forty-two books of poetry and facilitates three international Zoom poetry critique groups. He posts daily on Instagram, and over 12,400 poets follow him online. He is an entrant for the 2024 Pulitzer Prize for Poetry. Elliot has won first place in the Poets Corner Poetry Contest and has published numerous poems in assorted anthologies.

To see all of his books of poetry, crime novels and more, go to **www.CreativeFiction.net**

The Author, RR

I never set out to write, but like many, life kidnapped me, put me on a ship on a wide, choppy ocean and I developed sailor's legs.

Over my 39 year career with the State of NJ in IT and energy, I developed into a professional business and technical writer and contracts manager for IT equipment and software, electricity and natural gas, even solar and wind.

Now it's 2025, I'm 74, still have some intelligence, can type, so I write "just because." I hope you write your story/poems/essays blogs etc. and publish. That's my goal, to tell everyone they should—for no cost at all.

I've critiqued 3,000+ pieces in weekly writing workshops, written 275 essays published on Bahai Teachings.org , edited and published 15 books for others, revealed a raw bipolar memoir, four poetry books and co-authored two volumes on running small businesses.

Imagine what you'll do.

I'm an active member of the Bahá'í Faith and have served in multiple capacities. During my NJ career I received three National Awards, Regional, State, and others for our programs. In my locality, I've served as a volunteer dispute resolution mediator for 24 years for the courts, and on my town's Environmental Advisory Commission for seven. I'm the publicity director for the Friends of our local public library.

I married my high school sweetheart; we have two incredible adult children and enjoy sumptuous times with our grandchildren.

Writing and sailing the seven seas with my spirit and fingers never stops. It's a precious world worthy of keeping peaceful.

Caio and best wishes

Rod

Contact me at 1950ablia@gmail.com
Or www.rodneyrichards.info

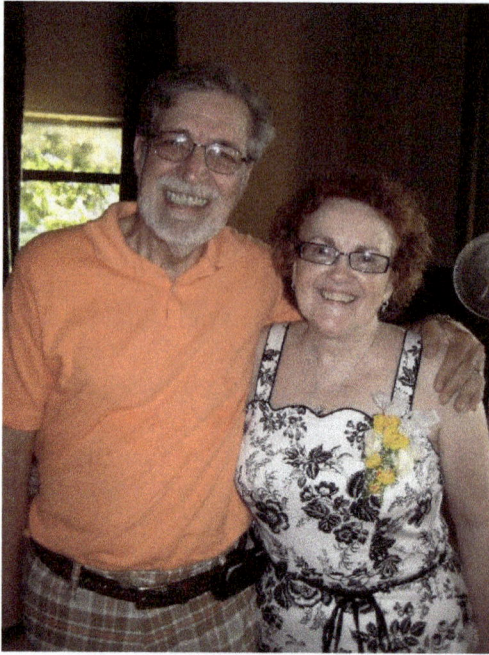

A Poet Sings Poems   by RR

Already written my best poem,
    don't recognize it as perfection
    it's in the eye of the beholder
Hundreds typed, revised, edited, formatted
    reside in the cloud of my OneDrive's belly
    available at filename touch
If one moves me, okay to publish
    for the heck of it
    someone else will be judge, jury

Why Religion? Why Bahá'í?

The Bahá'í Faith was beyond obscure when I first heard of it in 1969. I lived in a shared-rent, six-bedroom home in the well-to-do West End section of Trenton, NJ. The house was so big; we played tennis against the walls of our dining room, had a library with pocket doors, six bedrooms, a back stairway from the kitchen to the 2nd floor, a surrounding porch, and Tommy's '63 Jaguar engine in the empty full-length basement.

Drugs and alcohol flowed, gifts from our regular pusher, Charlie, who visited often with free junk. Two of the guys and Margaret were in Trenton State College. Two other guys worked. I spoon-fed meals to geriatric patients at Trenton Psychiatric Hospital.

It was bellbottoms, sandals, dashikis, long hair time, party time, and beat the draft time by going to college. I was soaking it all in. One evening a guy named Ted stopped over to see one of the guys, but they weren't there. I led him into the library and stayed to be polite. We chatted and he mentioned Bahá'í.

I grew up with all the Catholic cliches and rites and believed God sent divine Messengers, although knew little about others. But to listen to Teddy tell it, religion seemed alive and worthwhile, even exciting.

Instantly attracted and curious, I peppered questions until Janet came over for our date. She knew Teddy as an ex-senior classmate, so she sat and listened too.

Truth can only be discovered when open to it.

The rest is our history and story. Jan and I attended talks called firesides at homes of area Bahá'is. During months of inquiry, they gave us books and pamphlets to read, even personal prayer books. We traveled to events around the state, read more books, and met tons of folks at places like the Teaneck Cabin. The people were normal, kind, and loving.

In July 1970, we both joined. We found truth in an odd, unexpected, surprising way. We didn't know we were searching and have been happy and grateful since.

Thanks for being such good readers and listeners.

Caio, Rod

INFORMATION ON THE BAHÁ'Í FAITH

The Faith teaches unity, oneness, peace, cooperation, love for every human being, and of God. It is the same spirit contained in the scriptures of all of God's holy messengers, updated for each age in which They appear.

'Abdu'l-Bahá, Bahá'u'lláh's Son, said this about what it means to be a Bahá'í: "…be the embodiment of all human perfections."

Contact Information: 1-800-22-UNITE (800-228-6483)
U.S. Bahá'í website https://www.bahai.us/

Bahá'í World website https://www.bahai.org/

Find Bahá'í quotations at https://www.bahai.org/library/

www.bahaiteachings.org contains thousands of essays on innumerable topics by varied writers, including mine.

Contact me

Write to me at 1950ablia@gmail.com
    Include the subject, your full name, and your email address. Contact me here if in need of editing, polishing, formatting, and publishing services. Check my website at www.rodneyrichards.info

Thanks for reading!
    I'd be grateful if you left a review on those sites you frequent. Your interest and views make a difference.
    Find me too on Facebook at **rodneywriter** or on Instagram at **rrichardswriter**. Check my website blog for writers, **Write with Authority 2**.
    Thanks for your support!